TURTLES

Published by Creative Education, Inc., 123 South Broad Street, Mankato, Minnesota
56001

Printed by permission of Wildlife Education, Ltd.

Library of Congress Cataloging-in-Publication Data

Biel, Timothy L.
Turtles / by Timothy Levi Biel.
p.   cm. — (Zoobooks)
Originally published: San Diego, CA: Wildlife Education, 1988 (Zoobooks; v. 5, no.
8).
Includes index.
Summary: Identifies many types of turtles, describing physical characteristics, habits,
and habitats.
ISBN 0-88682-411-7
1. Turtles—Juvenile literature. [1. Turtles.] I. Title. II. Series: Zoo books (Mankato,
Minn.)
QL666.C5B47   1991   597.92—dc20   91-9948 CIP AC

TURTLES

This Book Created by
Quality Publications, Inc.

Written by
Timothy Levi Biel

Editorial Consultant
John Bonnett Wexo

Zoological Consultant
Charles R. Schroeder, D.V.M.
Director Emeritus
San Diego Zoo &
San Diego Wild Animal Park

Scientific Consultants
Dr. Peter C.H. Pritchard, Ph.D.
Florida Audubon Society

Dr. Jeanne Mortimer, Ph.D.
Zoological Department,
University of Florida

Creative Education

Photographic Credits

Cover: Zig Leszcynski (Animals Animals); **Page Sixs and Seven:** Joe McDonald (Tom Stack & Assoc.); **Page Nine: Top Left,** Jeff Foott; **Top Right,** Cyril Toker (Alpha/FPG); **Pages Ten and Eleven:** David M. Dennis (Tom Stack & Assoc.); **Page Twelve:** Jane Burton (Bruce Coleman, Ltd.); **Page Thirteen:** Tom McHugh (Photo Researchers); **Pages Fourteen and Fifteen:** Erwin and Peggy Bauer (Bruce Coleman, Inc.); **Page Sixteen:** (Alpha/FPG); **Page Seventeen: Middle,** Anthony Bannister (Natural History Photos); **Bottom,** Paul Kuhn (Tom Stack & Assoc.); **Page Eighteen:** David Hughes (Bruce Coleman, Ltd.); **Page Nineteen: Top,** (Carnegie Museum of Natural History); **Bottom,** David Hughes (Bruce Coleman, Ltd.); **Page Twenty:** Keith Gillett (Animals Animals); **Page Twenty-One:** Bob McKeever (Tom Stack & Assoc.); **Page Twenty-Two and Inside Back Cover:** Ron and Valerie Taylor (Ardea London).

Art Credits

Main Illustrations by Rebecca Bliss; **Sidebar Illustrations** by Walter Stuart.

Our Thanks To: Ed Hamilton (San Diego Bionomics); Dr. Greg Pragle (Department of Herpetology, San Diego Museum of Natural History); Dr. Robert Bezy (Herpetology Section, Natural History Museum of Los Angeles County); Michael Kassem; Tom Clark; Pamela Stuart.

This book is dedicated with deepest love and gratitude to Melanie Biel.

Contents

Turtles are strange looking creatures. The shells on their backs are like roofs that they carry with them wherever they go. No other animals in the world have shells quite like these, and they have been the secret of the turtles' success for millions of years.

Like dinosaurs, turtles are primitive reptiles that first appeared on earth about 200 million years ago. These early turtles had smaller shells than most modern turtles, so they couldn't cover their heads. But as dangerous predators began to appear, many turtles gradually developed larger shells, so their heads would fit inside.

Today, dinosaurs are no longer roaming the earth. But turtles just keep plodding along, even though they haven't changed much over the years. Their shells give them excellent protection, and this has helped them adapt to all but the coldest parts of the world. They can live in jungles, mountains, rivers, deserts, and even in the sea.

There are now more than 200 different species of turtles in the world. They range in size from tiny Speckled Tortoises, which weigh less than one-half pound (220 grams), to monstrous Leatherback Turtles, which can weigh *1500 pounds* (680 kilograms)! Most of these species fit into one of three main groups: *freshwater turtles*, *sea turtles*, or *tortoises* (TOR-tuss-uz).

Freshwater turtles live in rivers or ponds. They have webbed feet and flat shells. Sea turtles live in the sea. They have powerful flippers for swimming long distances. Tortoises are a special group of turtles that live on dry land. Most of them have shells that are shaped like a dome. And they have thick, heavy legs for walking.

A few turtles, like the one pictured at right, do not fit in any of these groups. They can swim like freshwater turtles, but they spend a lot of time on land, like tortoises. Scientists call these turtles *semi-terrestrial* (SEM-eye ter-REST-re-ull), which means "partly-land dwelling."

Some species of turtles probably live near you. You may find them living in a local pond, or in some nearby woods. And if people don't disturb them, they can go on living there for a long time. Some turtles even live to be a hundred years old!

6

DIAMONDBACK TERRAPIN

A turtle's shell is part of its skeleton. It cannot be removed from the turtle's body any easier than you could remove *your* skeleton from *your* body. What makes the turtle's skeleton so different is that its ribs and backbone are attached to flat, bony plates. These plates form a wonderful shelter that surrounds the turtle's body and keeps it safe from predators.

Of course, this skeleton also shapes the rest of the turtle's body. For example, its legs must stick out sideways in order to fit beneath the shell. With its bowed legs and bulky shell, the turtle is very slow and awkward, at least on land.

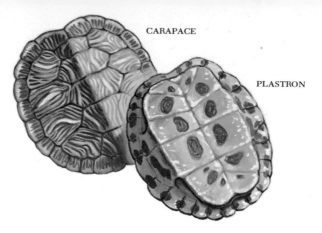

Every turtle shell has a top and a bottom. The top part is called a *carapace* (CARE-uh-pace), and the bottom is known as a *plastron* (PLASS-tron).

People and most animals have their shoulders and hips *outside* their ribs. But turtles have them *inside* their ribs, so their shell can cover the rest of the body. Can you find a shoulder on this turtle?

SHOULDER

Most turtle shells are covered with hard *scales*. Like fingernails, these scales are made of *keratin* (CARE-uh-tin), and they grow out of an extremely thin layer of "skin." Also, a turtle can feel pressure through its shell in the same way that you feel pressure when you press on your fingernail.

BONE

"SKIN"

SCALES

Turtle shells are not all alike. Some can close completely around the head and body, while others can't. A tortoise's shell, for example, barely fits over its head, so its face is not protected.

A turtle's legs may move slowly, but its neck can move with lightning speed. The neck muscles are extremely flexible, and the skin is very loose. This allows the turtle to pull its whole neck inside the shell in case of danger.

To pull their heads under their shells, most turtles fold their necks in an "S" shape, as shown at right.

HAWKSBILL TURTLE

For its size, the sea turtle has a very small shell. It barely covers the turtle's back, and provides no protection to the head or legs.

Turtles have no teeth. But their jaws have a hard covering, just like a bird's beak. The edges of these jaws are very sharp, so that turtles can eat many different kinds of food. The Painted Turtle at left is using its jaws to chop leaves.

The jaws of every turtle look different. Some have sharp points that are used like teeth for grabbing prey. Mexican Mud Turtles may even use these points to grab frogs.

9

This Pig-Nosed Softshell Turtle, and some other turtles, have a shell covered with a leathery skin instead of horny plates. This gives their carapace a round and soft appearance.

11

Fresh water is the place where most turtles live. There are many different kinds of freshwater turtles in the world. Some of them are tiny, like the little Spotted Turtles that are often sold in pet shops. Others can get quite large, like the Snapping Turtles shown here.

These turtles find most of their food in the water. Many of them eat fish and other animals, which they catch in a number of different ways. Big Snapping Turtles, like the one at right, sometimes even try to sneak up on ducks.

Freshwater turtles can be found in warm tropical streams as well as northern ponds that may freeze in the winter. This is remarkable because turtles—like all reptiles—are *cold-blooded*. In other words, their body temperature rises and falls with the temperature of their surroundings. So freshwater turtles must use their surroundings in many ways to keep from getting too hot or too cold, as you see below.

TERRAPIN

Like you, turtles have to breathe air. But they don't need nearly as much oxygen as you do. In fact, a turtle can stay under water for hours without breathing!

① ②

On cold days, the water may be warmer than the land, so the turtles stay in the water. If the water itself gets too cold, they dig burrows in the mud ③. Inside their burrows, turtles may go into a deep sleep that lasts for months.

③

On sunny days, turtles climb out of the water to warm up on a rock or log ①. When they get too warm, they dive back into the water ②.

12

The Common Snapping Turtle is only about half as large as its cousin, the Alligator Snapping Turtle. But it is a more aggressive hunter. It has extremely powerful jaws, and once they close around an animal, there is no escape. This allows the Snapping Turtle to capture large fish—and even ducks, occasionally.

The head of a *matamata* (MAT-uh-MAT-uh) is like a vacuum cleaner. This strange-looking turtle from South America hides in murky water, where its reddish color makes it hard to see. When fish swim near, it sucks them in. It does this by stretching out its long neck and opening its huge mouth. Water immediately rushes in, and the fish is pulled in with it.

MATAMATA

The Alligator Snapping Turtle is a big, lazy turtle. It can be almost 4 feet long (90 centimeters) and weigh as much as 200 pounds (90 kilograms). This turtle just lies in muddy water where fish can't see it. When it gets hungry, it opens its mouth and wiggles its bright red tongue. Fish often mistake this tongue for a worm and swim right inside the turtle's gaping mouth. Snap! Just like that, the turtle has its meal.

13

Desert Tortoises enjoy the desert flowers that bloom in the spring as much as people do. While people are happy to see the colorful cactus flowers, the turtles are glad to *eat* them!

14

Tortoises are even slower than most other turtles. It takes a tortoise 5 hours just to walk one mile (1.6 kilometers)! But it doesn't need to move any faster.

It doesn't have to run fast to find food, because it eats plants. And with its shell to protect it, it has no fear of predators. In fact, most tortoises live in dry places where it helps to move slowly. If they tried to carry their heavy shells any faster, they would just get hot, tired, and thirsty.

Tortoises usually lead slow, quiet, and peaceful lives. There is very little that frightens or excites them. Occasionally, however, male tortoises get excited enough to fight over a female, as the two Desert Tortoises are doing below.

GIANT LAND TORTOISE

Most tortoises weigh less than 10 pounds (4.5 kilograms). But a Giant Land Tortoise may weigh *600 pounds* (275 kilograms)! That's about as much as three large men.

TORTOISE

Watching two male tortoises fight is like watching a movie in slow motion. The tortoises push each other with their shells until one of them gets tipped on its back. A fight like this may last for hours.

16

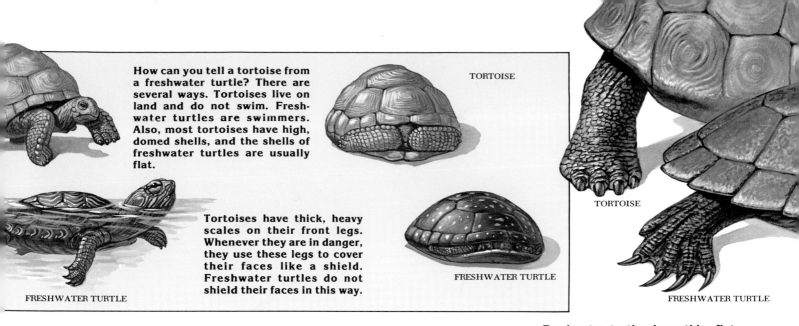

How can you tell a tortoise from a freshwater turtle? There are several ways. Tortoises live on land and do not swim. Freshwater turtles are swimmers. Also, most tortoises have high, domed shells, and the shells of freshwater turtles are usually flat.

TORTOISE

Tortoises have thick, heavy scales on their front legs. Whenever they are in danger, they use these legs to cover their faces like a shield. Freshwater turtles do not shield their faces in this way.

FRESHWATER TURTLE

TORTOISE

FRESHWATER TURTLE

FRESHWATER TURTLE

Freshwater turtles have thin, flat legs that are built for swimming. Tortoises have round, sturdy legs for walking on land. Because they live on land, tortoises do not have webbing between their toes like freshwater turtles do. Finally, a tortoise's back foot has only 4 toes, while a freshwater turtle's has 5.

LEOPARD TORTOISE

Many animals cannot survive in dry places because they can't find enough water. But tortoises get all the water they need by eating cactus and other plants that store moisture.

DESERT TORTOISES

In a fight, the tortoise that gets tipped over loses. And if it can't get back on its feet, it could lose its life! Left out in the hot sun, a tortoise will quickly get too hot and die.

Many tortoises live in underground burrows where they are protected from the weather. Gopher Tortoises are only about one foot long (30 centimeters), but they often dig tunnels that are *25 or 30 feet* long (7.–9 meters). These tunnels are like "apartments" that the tortoises share with gophers, toads, and other "neighbors."

Mysterious sea turtles have been roaming the world's oceans for millions of years. They were there at the time of the dinosaurs, and they are still there today. Yet until recently, scientists knew very little about them. They were rarely seen, except when they came to shore to mate and lay their eggs. Then they would disappear again into the sea.

However, with the aid of modern radio and satellite equipment, scientists are beginning to solve some of the mysteries of the sea turtle. They now know that these turtles travel in regular migration routes, some of them for thousands of miles. And every two or three years, they return to the same beaches where they hatched as babies. There are still mysteries to be solved, though. For example, no one knows how these turtles can make such long voyages and still find their way back to the same beaches time after time.

Millions of years ago, the ancestors of sea turtles lived on land. But today, sea turtles are completely adapted to life at sea. For example, the bones that once formed the turtle's toes have become extremely long. And instead of forming separate toes, they work together to form a big flipper.

PACIFIC RIDLEY TURTLES

Near a beach in Costa Rica, thousands of Pacific Ridley Turtles arrive at about the same time every year to mate. When all the females haul themselves onto shore to lay their eggs, they practically cover the whole beach! They may even do this in the daytime, although like most sea turtles, they usually lay their eggs at night.

Many turtle shells have beautifully colored scales. But none are as thick and durable as the Hawksbill Turtle's (above). For this reason, people use its scales to make "tortoiseshell" combs and jewelry. Unfortunately, for hundreds of years there were no limits on hunting these beautiful sea turtles. And today, they are seriously endangered.

Sea turtles have changed very little since the days when dinosaurs roamed the earth. In fact, the Leatherback Turtle (above) looks a lot like its ancestor (shown below).

ARCHELON

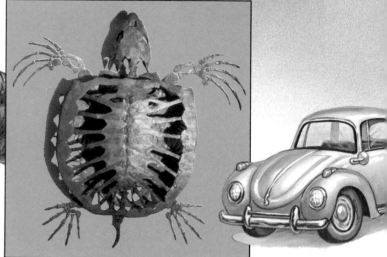

As far as we know, the largest sea turtle that ever lived was *Archelon* (ARK-uh-lon). Scientists have found skeletons of this giant sea turtle that are about 10 feet long (3 meters) from head to tail. They estimate that it must have weighed about *two tons* (1800 kilograms). In other words, Archelon was about the size of a small car!

Sea turtles can "fly" through the water. They are such powerful swimmers that they can reach speeds up to 15 miles per hour (24 kilometers per hour). That's about 75 times faster than a tortoise can walk!

Ⓐ

GREEN TURTLE

Ⓑ

Sea turtles get a lot of salt from the ocean water they drink Ⓐ. But if they take in too much salt, they could die. So they get rid of the extra salt by shedding big, salty tears Ⓑ.

A sea turtle's shell does not cover its head and legs. This makes it easier for the sea turtle to swim, but it has lost some valuable protection. So the sea turtle has thick, scaly skin on its head and legs. This skin protects it like a leather coat and hood.

19

A young turtle's life is full of danger. And like most reptiles, it gets no protection from its mother. In fact, it never sees her. The mother turtle buries her eggs in the ground and then leaves them to hatch by themselves. Many of the eggs will not hatch, however, because animals and people find them and eat them.

The baby turtles that do hatch are called *hatchlings*, and they face even more problems. On these pages, you will see how baby sea turtles hatch and what problems they may face. Like all hatchlings, the first thing they must do is dig their way out of an underground nest. This may take a few days, or even *a few weeks!* Then they must find a safe place to hide. But before they reach safety, many of the hatchlings are caught by hungry predators.

A mother sea turtle comes ashore long enough to lay her eggs and cover them up. Then she returns to the sea. Sea turtles are very awkward on land. They can only move by dragging their heavy bodies over the sand, leaving an unusual trail behind them.

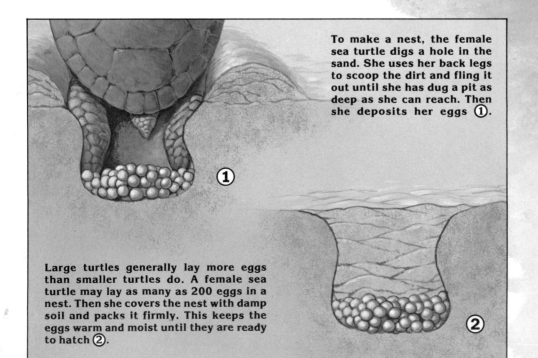

To make a nest, the female sea turtle digs a hole in the sand. She uses her back legs to scoop the dirt and fling it out until she has dug a pit as deep as she can reach. Then she deposits her eggs ①.

Large turtles generally lay more eggs than smaller turtles do. A female sea turtle may lay as many as 200 eggs in a nest. Then she covers the nest with damp soil and packs it firmly. This keeps the eggs warm and moist until they are ready to hatch ②.

Sea turtle eggs hatch two or three months after they are laid. Then the hatchlings dig their way out of their nests and try to get to the water as quickly as possible. But many of them never make it. They are caught by gulls, crabs, and other predators before they ever get there. And once they are in the water, young sea turtles still have to watch for sharks and other fish that like to eat them.

Even though sea turtle eggs are buried deep in the sand, they aren't always safe from animals or people. Some people, like the man above, find their nests and dig up the eggs.

The reason sea turtles lay so many eggs is that very few hatchlings live long enough to become adults. Of all the hatchlings in a nest, only one or two may live to adulthood.

Scientists aren't sure how sea turtle hatchlings know where to go, but as soon as they get above ground, they head straight for the sea. Then they may disappear for more than 20 years, until they return to the same beaches to mate and have young of their own.

The future of turtles once seemed secure. For millions of years, their shells were all the protection they needed. Today, however, they need a different kind of protection, which only people can give them. Turtles are facing many of the same problems that other wild animals face. Some of them have been overhunted, while others are threatened by pollution, destruction of their habitat, and the loss of important food sources.

About two hundred years ago, Giant Tortoises lived on many tropical islands. Now, because of overhunting, they are only found in two places in the world. Also in recent years, hotels and resorts have been built on many beaches where sea turtles once nested. Pesticides and other chemical wastes have polluted rivers and streams where freshwater turtles once lived. Entire forests have been chopped down where Wood Turtles and Box Turtles once roamed.

As a result, many species of turtles are disappearing from the world. Fortunately, some people are already working hard to save them. Lawmakers have passed laws to prevent the hunting of endangered turtles. Organizations like the World Wildlife Fund have sponsored projects to protect their eggs. And zoos have bred rare turtles in captivity. Yet these efforts are just a beginning. Much more must be done to give turtles the kind of protection they need.

This was once a secluded beach where thousands of sea turtles could have laid their eggs. Today, many of the world's tropical beaches look like this, and they are no longer suitable places for mother sea turtles to nest.

Loggerhead Turtles and other sea turtles spend their entire lives in the sea. But they must come to shore to lay their eggs. When they do, people sometimes collect their eggs. This means that fewer turtles are hatched and this is why many sea turtle species are endangered.

Index

DATE DUE